# THE SECOND HOME

*poems by*

# Vasiliki Katsarou

*Finishing Line Press*
Georgetown, Kentucky

# THE SECOND HOME

Copyright © 2023 by Vasiliki Katsarou
ISBN 979-8-88838-274-5 First Edition
All rights reserved under International and Pan-American Copyright Conventions. No part of this book may be reproduced in any manner whatsoever without written permission from the publisher, except in the case of brief quotations embodied in critical articles and reviews.

## ACKNOWLEDGMENTS

Thanks to the editors of the following journals and anthologies in which these poems first appeared:

*River Heron Review*: "White Iron Bird"
*Ergon: Greek/American Arts and Letters*: "Ekta-chrome"
*Schuylkill Valley Journal*: "Daughter after a Detail" and "Apricots"
*Rabbit Ears: TV Poems* (NYQ Books): "Season Four" as "The Bachelor Season Four"
*Literary Mama*: "Em–Oh–Em"
*Painted Bride Quarterly*: "Waited" and "The Future Arrives as a Redhead"
*ONE ART: a journal of poetry*: "The Branch"
*NOON: Journal of the Short Poem*: "The First Summer"

Publisher: Leah Huete de Maines
Editor: Christen Kincaid
Cover Art: Wassily Kandinsky, detail from *The Green Women*, Art
    Collection 4 / Alamy Stock Photo
Author Photo: A. Lutkus
Cover Design: Elizabeth Maines McCleavy

Order online: www.finishinglinepress.com
    also available on amazon.com

Author inquiries and mail orders:
Finishing Line Press
PO Box 1626
Georgetown, Kentucky 40324
USA

# Table of Contents

White Iron Bird ............................................................................ 1

Ekta-chrome .............................................................................. 2

Daughter after a Detail ............................................................. 4

Season Four .............................................................................. 5

Apricots ..................................................................................... 6

We Would Wed Our Words ..................................................... 8

Germinal ................................................................................. 10

Em–Oh–Em ............................................................................ 11

Waited ..................................................................................... 12

Change, but Who's Counting ................................................ 13

beloved boy ............................................................................ 15

The Branch ............................................................................. 16

The First Summer .................................................................. 17

The Future Arrives as a Redhead ......................................... 18

Notes ....................................................................................... 19

Additional Acknowledgments .............................................. 20

*for Angeliki and Stathi*

## White Iron Bird

When the child was young
and not yet strong
his grandma gifted him
with sage tests of his mettle
wings of paper money
amounting to his age
just to see him choose
among the flora
a folly to his measure.

In the first greenhouse of his life
his child's fist
settled upon a small white iron bird
classical in form, *poulaki mou*
Heavy and white,
heavier than thought
or hand could hold.

And when the time came
to pay for his choice,
he wasn't sold.
To hand over five paper wings
or the cold form of *poulaki*
perched in his palm?
Each fistful weighed equally.

To choose the beautiful thing
or its ephemeral wing,
to wait for something in us
to be released.

## Ekta-chrome

I.

man takes a woman
on a wedding trip
before I was born

last look upon home,
a café on the village square,
the field, its harvest of exile

pellucid Pelasgia
partial coinage
of a man-made image

or something like this
tangible language, this audible curve,
this emotionese

he left me
this ring
of partial glimpses


II.

the way I see it
I was left
to translate him

lift his disembodied eye
to my eye, find no archive of anecdota
but shed and shadow

self recognition in this
Cézannesque square: basket of fruit, sun-dappled wall—
I set my sepia-toned pastorals

against his transparency: modern markers of industry,
café tray, glass-bottled sodas, metal ashcan
are what I sought to leave out


III.

he left me
this ring
of partial glimpses

the way I see it
I was left
to translate him

"apple, o apple of my eye,"
he called me
*matia mou,* you who are my eyes—

why Ekta-chrome? I pressed him,
paper is ephemeral, he thought
*slide film is better, it'll last*

last, last little pools of memory
until this cold water
shall trickle
        over

### Daughter after a Detail

>after Anthony Van Dyck's *James, Seventh Earl of Derby, His Lady and Child*

Her plaited hands
her dress is lava
what hardens and is hidden
in a lace apron
in lace like ice, like frost, like flakes

her eyes hold a secret
her pearls are precious,
mouthless teeth ground down to perfection

her mother is satin, is silk,
is static, a guide for hiding
her own self-
making

the daughter is lava
molten fire forms her skirts
she skirts flaming mire
keeps her head above the fire

her lips will unpurse
in time

**Season Four**

the girls sway and swish
in silk, feathers, and paint

it is the season of peacock
blue and green

and the beau stands firm,
bathed in tropical moisture
eyes glassy and X-rayed—

just because years later
the artifice of that season
seems garish

and you are tempted
to pick apart your house
piece by piece

why not spare the glue and the screw
and let the whole edifice stand?

## Apricots

They stand frozen
in the family backyard
not too tall, not too short

two teenagers stranded
one from the other

apricot trees
planted by my father
to remind him of faraway home

the bitterness of waiting
for that yearly handful
of hard green knobs

and why it was rarely the sweetness of fruit,
the velvet cheek in his hand,
juice dripping down the chins

Were they the same
sex? Did the bees avoid them?

eventually blossoms appeared
but the ripening always evaded
his impatience

Did he rue the work?

*

Apricot-scented sense of waste-not
want-not

he'd say he was "all used up"
by the time he turned forty,

and so I was born,
first fruit of his later used-up years

now he's gone
left the apricot trees to stand alone
in every season

as all that sweetness
drip,
        drip,
                drips
onto a velvet floor

## We Would Wed Our Words

i. *when dinner is fast*

in the second home
no dinner is served
without a sidebar on shipbuilding,
oil excavation, or stainless steel

I only mimic
lurching jocularity
thrown elbows

this damn banter:
four minds race to beat
the laggard heart

no rejoinder here
shall ever go unrejoindered

all politics is proxy
when your issue is your issue
excuses of the apolitical
are further fodder for folderol


ii. *generation gap*

rusty waters
weave through the holler
flooded forks
and minded gaps

deep wood recedes
down a steep slope
thunder lurks here
behind every hilltop

iii. *we would wed our words*

if language is static
it is to prevent us from hearing a true signal

if language is a tool
to wedge us into an economy of wants

why yes, there is an endless supply
of demand


iv. *take leave(s)*

absorb summer's light
take to the air and give form
and an edge
then be sent

        hurtling down from the treetops

they lie
on the ground
palms up, veins up

stop me cold
with their gold

beggar delight
sweep me along
into some future
unknowingness

### *Germinal*

Green skin exhumes shadow from earth,
in spring suddenly
lines become volumes

there is no time outside
intervals measured by leaf and flicker

where once was porch and crag,
a steep leveling-off, its lines extending
toward infinity, or an arabesque of forgetting

now things must be accounted for
in at least three dimensions

no creeping obscurity can further flatten
what has surged into foreground, middle
ground, and back

**Em–Oh–Em**

Don't look for me where I once was
I left those wooded glades, cafés and libraries
changed my name to Em-Oh-Em
steeled myself against vomit and tears
dug in my heels
at the stove at the dishwasher
dragged my feet in the sandbox
followed the poison ivy lined path
to spot Godzilla approaching
or the tiniest LEGO piece
swept under the rug
until one day came the stop sign
and all the long detour
of your growing up—
all other signs set aside
just to be back in the thicket
of childhood—

I watch now as if from behind glass
the snowflakes shake off
their own snowflake
the tightly wound bud
of the peony bed
more vivid in memory
now that all those broken petals
are strewn across the front steps

**Waited**

you waited with me as the house
next door emptied of its guests,
then its owners, fairy tale turned animal farm

minted with ash and wishes
you were my kitchen elf
my second thought

my echo's echo
cocked ear, cracked oasis
your absorbent embered orbs

that morning of the supermoon
setting behind the barn
you were quiet, then quieter still

white fog settling into the hollows
and a thin coat of frost everywhere
and *this*, the simplest death

you trained me well, M.
I listen for your listening

## Change, but Who's Counting

housebound
a mother's gaze
is the hand that skims all
tidying tidying

the rooms themselves
secreting coins
nickels in pockets
pennies in old floorboards

when we were young
we had no source of income

surplus accumulated
until we amounted to something

seasons later
I am the house's wife
and there shall be an accounting

overturned into echo
into clatter

I haul my mined coins
to the bank,
hazard a guess as to value

push and push
a metallic river of years
through the slot…

stand by,
out pop

           two rusty nails

    an abandoned house-
key

          a baby molar

a horsehair brush

the machine dings
and prints receipt,

belated roulette of reality—
compound number,
relayed in wonder,

perhaps even asterisked

          delight

**beloved boy**

beloved boy
sun to my moon
moon to my son

your half smile
is history

your skin
is a fluted column of light

you house grandmothers
and ancestors
in your cheeks

**The Branch**

my mother leans in-
to the kitchen doorway
dressed in my old clothes

after hoeing and weeding
gleefully, she brandishes
a question, a branch—

wayward branch,
she found you jammed
inside the flowering azalea
hard by my front door

how she pulled you,
broken thorny dead thing
from the shrub of flowers
and offered you to me

misbegotten bouquet of dry bark,
and how tickled by my lapse
she stands in wait—

how it mars the face
of the house
I show my neighbors

how the unsightly
has indeed hovered
at my doorstep

and I willfully
blind to its presence
came and went
and never once stopped
to thank her

**The First Summer**

the first summer, we found cuttlefish bones on the beach

the second summer, a pirate's bounty of silver sea stones

the third summer, white cats in a basket, a mother's prayer

the fourth summer, a cask of winds: *vorinós, meltémi, capellátos, kareklás*

soon after came the rain and the fasts

I lost my hat

turned up at a crossroads

at the center

of the center of the island town

## The Future Arrives as a Redhead

They talk of mothers in law
but not of outlaw daughters

her sun and her moon is our son
her cool paleness, reflected

in an eye that looks like mine,
follows her curves along the shoreline

her hair like copper coils
from beneath a straw hat

a Maisie or Daisy, a woman of Stem
for whom we stem talk of servers,

thumbprint keys, on an ancient island
now we are all code-changers

the future arrives as a redhead
green, green love lays a glove

on us, we no longer count
in threes, a quaver

sounds, and the future
all sharps and flats

## Notes

*White Iron Bird*
In Greek, *poulaki* indicates the diminutive "little bird," but is also a euphemistic word for male genitalia. Colloquially, *poulaki mou* also means "my dear little child."

*Ekta-chrome*
The Kodak color positive or slide film that produces a positive image on a transparent base. The word is coined of course from two Greek words: *ekta* (beyond) and *chrome* (color).

This poem is for my father Petros, engineer and photographer. Pelasgia is the town in Greece where both of my parents were raised.

*Germinal*
I have the French word in mind, *Germinal*, seventh month of the French Revolutionary calendar.

*The First Summer*
Cycladic island winds: the latter two are humorous—*capellátos*, wind that blows hats off; *kareklás*, wind that knocks chairs down.

**Additional Acknowledgments**

I dedicate this book to the memory of my beloved Aunt Angeliki and Uncle Stathi, who provided a second home to me in Athens, in all my years of growing up, and also as an adult, when I lived in France. Loving, elegant, hardworking and creative, they are part of a bygone Athens. I will miss them greatly. May their memory be eternal.

In New Jersey, I'm fortunate to enjoy a supportive community of fellow artists. I'm grateful to John Timpane who took time to read a longer version of this work and who made insightful suggestions. I also thank MaryAnn L. Miller for the attention she gave to these poems. Thanks also to Dean Kostos for a close reading of this work. Gratitude to John Wall Barger for his friendship and critical eye.

My thanks go out to Hunterdon Art Museum, and to the members of the Hunterdon Poets Workshop for entrusting me with their poetry. Thank you to Hayden Saunier, and members of the poetry performance cooperative *No River Twice*, for camaraderie and opportunities to read from this chapbook.

Thank you to artist writer poet choral singer Ravenna Taylor for sisterhood.

I'm deeply honored and grateful to the poet Dennis Nurkse—for his friendship, encouragement, and for his beautiful poetry.

These poems spring from an ongoing dialogue with my loves, Tony Lutkus and Paul Lutkus.

Vasiliki Katsarou was raised in Massachusetts by Greek-born parents. She is a poet, editor, independent curator, and teaching artist. Honored as a Geraldine R. Dodge poet, her poems have been published widely, and internationally, including in *Poetry Daily, Otoliths, Tiferet: A Journal of Spiritual Literature, Wild River Review, Literary Mama, La Vague Journal, Contemporary American Voices, NOON: Journal of the Short Poem* (Japan), Corbel Stone Press' *Contemporary Poetry Series* (U.K.), *Regime Journal* (Australia), *Mediterranean Poetry* (Denmark), and in *Mandragoras* (in Greek translation). Her work has been nominated for a Pushcart Prize. She is the author of a full-length poetry collection, *Memento Tsunami*, and a chapbook, *Three Sea Stones*. She is also co-editor of two contemporary poetry anthologies: *Eating Her Wedding Dress,* and *Dark as a Hazel Eye*, published by Ragged Sky Press. A Phi Beta Kappa graduate of Harvard University, she holds an MFA from Boston University. Since moving to New Jersey in 2002, Vasiliki has curated and organized numerous public poetry and art events at galleries and museums, and founded a long-running poetry reading series in Lambertville, NJ. Her poems were part of a 2022 art exhibition at the contemporary art center ArtYard. As a filmmaker, her award-winning 35mm short film *Fruitlands 1843*, was featured at the Museum of Fine Arts Boston, the Harvard Film Archive, the Independent Film Project/Angelika Film Center, and at the Drama Film Festival in Greece. She is a Teaching Artist at Hunterdon Art Museum.

www.ingramcontent.com/pod-product-compliance
Lightning Source LLC
Chambersburg PA
CBHW022129090426
42743CB00008B/1070